INTRODUCTION

Thank you for purchasing the book "African Elephants Fun Facts and Fantastic Photos for Kids! Learn About African Animals."

With the help of this book, you will learn everything you need to know about African Elephants — from what they look like to what they eat. You will also learn what they are afraid of and so much more!

Turn the page now and enter the wonderful world of African Elephants!

CHAPTER 1
MEET THE AFRICAN
ELEPHANT

African Elephants Fun Facts and Fantastic Photos for Kids! Learn About African Animals

African Elephants Fun Facts and Fantastic Photos for Kids!
Learn About African Animals

TABLE OF CONTENTS

What are African Elephants?

African Elephants are the largest living mammals on land that are only found in Africa. They are called African Elephants because for some reason, their ears look a little bit like the African Continent. They come from the genus of Loxodonta, which means *oblique-sided tooth*.

African Elephants' trunks are used for breathing, smelling, taking care of children, and noticing if the ground is shaking. Trunks can also be used for grasping objects and drinking water.

There are two types of African Elephants: The African Bush Elephant which is the largest mammal on land, and the African Forest Elephant, which is the third largest. They are all found in the Eastern, Southern, and Western regions of Africa.

African Elephants are important in keeping nature in balance because without them, African forests would just be full of unnecessary trees and dirt. It would definitely be sad living in a world without the beauty and grace of elephants.

Baby Elephants

A baby elephant is called a calf, the same as baby goats and cattle, and usually weighs 100 kilograms at birth. Newly-born elephants are blind and suck their thumbs to feel comfortable and secure. They cannot think and decide for themselves yet, and that's why their mothers never let them wander too far.

Baby elephants are also born with tusks. These tusks fall out a year later and are replaced with permanent tusks, the same way baby teeth are replaced with permanent teeth.

When a mother elephant gives birth, elephants from her tribe form a circle around her. They do that to protect her. When the baby elephant is born, the other elephants help it stand up. Older elephants teach younger elephants to love and care for the baby until it can live life on its own. Now that's what you call a family!

Male Elephants

Also called *bulls*, male elephants usually roam around. They don't like the company of their fellow elephants too much and when they are ready to live alone, they wander the forests by themselves. However, some scientists say that in Kenya, some male elephants have at least one other male elephant as a best friend. They travel around the forests together, most of the time.

Male Elephants spray their urine on themselves when they feel like they are up for a fight. When they do this, it means that they are aggressive and it would be best to leave them alone. No one really knows when and why this happens.

Female Elephants

Female elephants are called *cows*. Unlike male elephants who are quite independent, females don't usually like being alone and like to be in the company of their families and friends. They feel comfortable living in a group with 15 other females. Mothers also ask their friends to take care of their babies so they have time to rest and produce milk.

As you have learned, when they are ready to give birth, it is important for them to be surrounded by a herd of female elephants so they would feel safe. Females like to have a lot of support and they also don't like to walk in the forests on their own.

Origin of the word Elephant

The word "Elephant" originated from the Greek word "Elephas" which means ivory. Elephants have Ivory Tusks and that's why they were named that way.

What do African Elephants look like?

They are often grayish brown with rough and thin body hair. They also have long trunks and tusks. Their trunks end with two opposing lips that never stop growing longer. They have thick bodies and really stocky legs. They also have four molars and a firm set of teeth, making it easy for them to chew and eat. They can grow up to 13 feet high and weigh up to 7,000 kilograms (or about 7,000 sacks of potatoes! Whew!). Unlike their relatives, African Elephants have boneless, muscular trunks.

The Height

The average male African Elephant weighs 5,500 kilograms while females weigh 2,700 kilograms. The average height of an African elephant is between 9 to 13 feet.

What do African Elephants like doing?

African Elephants are hungry most of the time so they do not sleep a lot. Instead, they usually look for food. They can walk far distances just to find food. Elephants eat a lot because they have to get the right nutrients to stay healthy and strong. They also like showering a lot since they are fond of water.

Skilled Smellers

Have you noticed that elephants have really long noses (or trunks)? Do you think they are good at smelling things? Well, they really are. Scientists say that even dogs are no match for elephants in telling one scent from another. Elephants can also smell something farther away than all other animals. If you can't imagine how amazing that is, first think about your dog. Everything your dog does, an elephant can do twice as good.

Intelligent Giants

Since elephants are so big, they also have huge brains. If your science teacher hasn't told you yet, animals with big brains are also super smart. How smart is an African Elephant? They're among the most intelligent mammals. Some scientists even say that elephants are just as brainy as monkeys and dolphins. Well, elephants might even be brighter since they have 11-pound brains. Are you sure that you are smarter than these intelligent giants?

Eating Machines

Some of the biggest elephants in the world weigh up to 16,500 tons, which means that they are definitely big eating machines. As you already know, elephants don't spend a lot of time sleeping instead they use their time for eating. They eat a lot in the morning and in the evening. They sleep for only a few hours in the afternoon. In fact, in just one day, they can already consume up to 50 gallons of water and around 170 kilos of vegetables!

While elephants always eat happily, they sometimes kill the trees they eat from. If you're wondering how this happens, just think about their trunks. Elephants use them as arms, reaching for the juiciest leaves. Since their trunks are like very muscular arms, they usually break several branches while they eat. Any tree that has many broken branches and almost no leaves will have a hard time staying alive.

African elephants also give other leaf-eating animals a hard time. Since they chow down on so many leaves, the elephants sometimes leave nothing for other creatures to eat. Some people who grow trees also tend to worry when elephants are near. They think that the massive mammals will eat everything in their gardens.

Weird Things that Elephants Eat

Even though elephants are huge, they do not eat animals. They are herbivores so they mostly feed on twigs, seed pods, fruits, barks, roots, and grass. Sometimes, they also eat flowers and almost every other kind of plants. Because of all the things that they eat, elephants produce large amounts of dung too. Yikes!

CHAPTER 2
THEIR FIGHTS AND FEARS

How do Elephants Defend Themselves?

Now that you know what elephants love, aren't you curious about what they hate? They hate their *predators.* Predators are animals that hunt and eat elephants. To scare away their natural enemies, like crocodiles and lions, elephants use their trunks by making loud noises. The elephants also use their trunks to fight their enemies when they have to.

Do elephants use their tusks to fight? Yes, they do. Elephants who want to protect their families and friends from ferocious animals sometimes charge with their tusks. Even the biggest and strongest mammals can be hurt by an elephant's pointed tusk. However, not all elephants are good at fighting and protecting themselves, since some of them have dull, curved tusks.

What are Elephants Afraid of?

If you have seen the film *"Dumbo"*, you might think that Elephants are afraid of mice. This is not true. Elephants are not afraid of mice but they are afraid of…Ants! It is said that ants are hated by all kinds of elephants. The majestic mammals get itchy and irritated whenever ants climb up their trunks. Since ants are so small, it's nearly impossible for elephants to get rid of them. Yikes!

African Elephants stay away from Acacia trees found in the Savannah because they believe that these are full of ants. They would rather eat other kinds of trees instead of being marched on by ants.

Aside from ants, elephants are also scared of bees. They don't go to fields that are full of beehives because they believe that the bees will sting and poison them.

Elephants and their Predators

Even if elephants are the biggest mammals on Earth, they have their own share of enemies and predators.

If elephants are not careful while staying in water, they might be attacked by crocodiles, especially if they are young and are not with their parents.

On land, lions and hyenas are the biggest enemies of elephants. Elephants may be big, but they can't run fast, unlike lions and hyenas. Hyenas look for young elephants and think of them as a feast, so elephants have to be extra careful when there are hyenas around.

Humans also harm elephants. Do you want to know why? It is because there are evil people who hunt and kill elephants just to get their tusks, selling those tusks for a lot of money. Some also destroy the forests where elephants live. This makes the elephants stressed and worried. The good thing is, destroying forests is now against the law. Anyone who is caught cutting down trees will be put in jail. It is important to keep elephants safe. If they are not treated the right way, elephants may be gone in a few years.

Escaping from Danger

Since they move slowly, African Elephants are lucky because there is enough room for them to go around, unlike Asian Elephants who are slowly losing their home.

African Elephants can find their way towards their tribe by walking through the grasslands. If their fellow elephants see them, it will be easy for them to escape from danger because predators don't attack elephants when they are with their tribe.

In case you find yourself being charged by elephants, you should stand still and watch their ears. If their ears are pointing outwards, it means that it is a mock charge and that they will not really attack you. Just stay where you are and move away once the elephants walk past you. If the ears are pointing in or back, shoo the elephant by making lots of noise. Remember not to run. If you do, the elephant will get angry. Just move quickly and climb a large tree if you can. Don't let the elephant know that you are afraid.

Aggressive African Elephants

It is usually the male elephants who become aggressive. This is because there are some chemicals in their bodies that make them nervous and angry when they are in the presence of other kinds of animals. They also become aggressive and frustrated when they are in stressful situations, like being in narrow places or not being able to eat well. Sometimes, when elephants are kept in zoos and are not well taken care of, they also become aggressive. They fight back when they think that people are threatening them.

Male elephants sometimes experience *musth*, making them feel like they need to hurt other animals. So, to be safe, don't go near male elephants on your own.

The elephants also become aggressive when they feel the need to avenge members of their tribe who were hurt or killed for no reason at all. Elephants are *clannish* — or very close to their families and relatives. Protecting their tribe is important to them. Elephants have very sharp memories so it's easy for them to remember if their family and friends have been hurt.

Shocking Displays

Not all elephants are lucky enough to live in their natural homes. Some are caught and placed in zoos or circuses. Because of this, the elephants become aggressive. And of course, there are people who tease the elephants, making them scared and angry at the same time.

Since elephants are wild animals, it's not easy for them to live in the zoo or in the circus. Being trained is also difficult for them. Not having the chance to eat as many times as they want to in a day is also tough. In some places, elephants are even used by people to help them beg for money in the streets or they are placed in animal shows. These are very bad things to do and may make the elephants sick. Of course, elephants that are not healthy live short lives.

CHAPTER 3
SIMILAR BUT DIFFERENT

Elephants and Humans: The Similarities

After learning so much about African Elephants, have you ever thought that humans and elephants are similar? We look different from them but there are a couple of things that make humans and elephants alike. We say "hello" as a way of greeting someone we know. Do you know that elephants do the same? They touch trunks to say "hello" to their families and friends.

Like people who miss someone they have not seen for quite some time, elephants miss their brood, too. Even after just a day of traveling, if an elephant comes back to its family, it is greeted with a lot of love and affection. Parents also take care of their children until they are ready to face life on their own (they're really like humans, aren't they?). This is because elephants also believe in the value of close families and that's why they cherish each other a lot.

People speak when they want to say something to each other and elephants make use of their trunks to create noises that will show fellow elephants how they feel and what they want to say. Elephants also shake the ground to talk to each other.

Here's another similarity between us and elephants – there are left- and right-handed people, and there are left- and right-tusked elephants. Elephants use their tusks to do a lot of things, but they don't use both of them. Some elephants like to use their left tusks while other elephants think it's better to use their right tusks.

African Elephants VS Asian Elephants

Here are the similarities and differences of African and Asian Elephants:

❖ African Elephants are bigger than Asian Elephants. Asian Elephants only weigh 3,000 to 6,000 kilos, while African Elephants usually weigh 4,000 to 7,000 kilos.

❖ An African Elephant's skin is rougher than that of an Asian Elephant's.

(Wrinkled skin of African Elephant)

AFRICAN ELEPHANTS

❖ African Elephants have 20 pairs of ribs while Asian Elephants have 21.

❖ African Elephants' ears are bigger and can reach backwards while the Asian Elephants' ears cannot.

❖ An Asian Elephant's back is straight while an African Elephant's is curved.

❖ An Asian Elephant's belly is usually sagging while an African Elephant's is slanted or point downwards.

❖ An African Elephant's head isn't crumpled the way an Asian Elephant's is. Also, an African Elephant's head does not have humps and dents while an Asian Elephant's head has all these.

❖ An Asian Elephant's teeth are packed close together while an African Elephant's teeth have spaces in between and are diamond-shaped.

❖ Female Asian Elephants do not usually have tusks, while both male and female African Elephants have tusks.

❖ An Asian Elephant's trunk is harder than that of an African Elephant's.

❖ African Elephants like to eat leaves while Asian Elephants love grass more than anything in the world.

❖ The tip of an African Elephant's trunk has two fingers while that of an Asian Elephant's only has one.

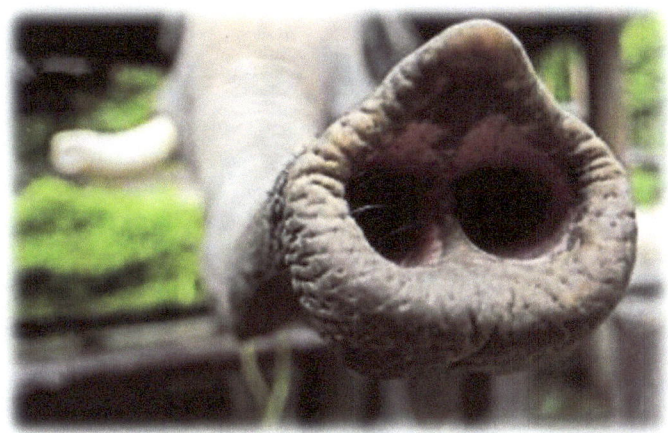

❖ An African Elephant has 4 or 5 toes on his forelegs and 3 or 4 on his hind legs, while an Asian Elephant has 5 toes on his forelegs and 4 or 5 toes on his hind legs.

❖ Asian Elephants can't run while African Elephants can run just a little bit.

❖ African Elephants use their tusks to dig the ground and fight their enemies. These tusks grow throughout their life. The tusks help them rest their trunks when they feel like the weight is already too heavy. After all, it's so hard to walk around all day with heavy trunks, so they definitely need some rest.

❖ African and Asian Elephants cannot form families together. So, there can never be any African-Asian Elephants. But in 1978, scientists tried making an African-Asian Elephant. A calf named "Motty" was born, but it died even though it was given a lot care.

CHAPTER 4
WEIRD, FUN, AND LITTLE-KNOWN FACTS

Elephants and Dogs: Best Friends?

While we may never really know if all elephants and dogs can be the best of friends, there is actually an elephant and a dog who are best friends and they live in South Carolina's Myrtle Beach Safari.

The elephant is Bubbles, who weighs 9,000 pounds and the dog's name is Bella, a Labrador Retriever. They seem like an odd pair but they love spending time with each other. They take walks and play in the water together.

Bubbles was adopted in 1983. He was given his own swimming pool at the safari in 2007. As for Bella, someone abandoned her and she found comfort in the company of Bubbles.

There have also been reports of elephants rescuing dogs, showing the world that they should not be feared all the time and that they are filled with kindness. You see, opposites do attract!

Weird Facts about African Elephants

Here are some weird but awesome facts about African Elephants:

❖ African Elephants have the longest period of pregnancy. Females carry their babies in their wombs for 22 months (that's almost two years), unlike humans who are only pregnant for 9 months!

❖ The elephants' feet act as cushions, making the majestic mammals feel comfortable while walking around. However, not all feet are the same: some have four toes, while some have five!

❖ Their head has many air pockets. There are also extra muscles found in their skull and neck which makes it easier for elephants to move their huge heads.

AFRICAN ELEPHANTS

❖ Unlike their ancestors, the mammoths, African Elephants are not hairy creatures. Hair just sometimes grows on their bodies and on their mouths and tails!

❖ African Elephant's trunk is strong enough to kill a lion. That's how powerful the gigantic creature is. African Elephants also have long lives. They can live up to 60 years in the wild!

Fun Facts

❖ Elephants don't like the feel and taste of peanuts. Even if they are in zoos, they are not given peanuts.

❖ Aside from humans, elephants are the only mammals that have chins!

❖ Elephants can recognize themselves in a mirror--just like magpies, dolphins, and apes!

AFRICAN ELEPHANTS

- ❖ Elephants actually weigh the same as the tongues of blue whales! Whoa!

- ❖ Asian Elephants have two feet on the ground most of the time, and that's why they cannot run.

- ❖ Some elephants in Kenya can actually mimic the sounds of trucks. Mimicry, or repeating what they hear or see, is one of their ways of learning.

- ❖ An elephant's trunk does not have bones — it is composed of over 150,000 muscles alone!

AFRICAN ELEPHANTS

❖ Elephants only sleep for around 2 hours each day! You will surely feel tired if you try that.

❖ African Elephants use their feet to know if the ground is mildly shaking. This means that they easily know if an earthquake is just around the corner.

❖ Some elephants actually have a sixth toe! This toe is actually a cartilage attached to their big toe.

❖ When a mother elephant bats a calf with her tail, it means that she wants to know that the calf is still following her.

❖ Sounds that elephants make are called rumbling.

❖ Humans don't usually hear elephant calls because their voices are too low and impossible for humans to hear. However, elephants can hear these calls even if they are 8 miles away!

AFRICAN ELEPHANTS

❖ The Largest Elephant on Earth weighed around 24,000 pounds and was 13 feet tall!

❖ Some elephants live more than 80 years!

Little-Known Facts

❖ Elephants sprinkle sand all over their bodies to keep themselves from being sunburned.

❖ Older elephants spend more time lying down than walking around the forests.

❖ The rock hyrax, a furry small mammal is considered as the elephant's closest living relative. You can usually find rock hyrax in the Arabian Peninsula and in the Sahara Desert in Africa. The rock hyrax looks like a mouse but it isn't related to rodents of any kind.

- ❖ In Kenya, some farmers protect their crops against elephants by placing beehives around their fields!

- ❖ When threatened, elephants make trumpeting sounds using their trunks to get the attention of their tribe.

- ❖ Elephants have 26 teeth in all.

- ❖ Elephants are India's national animal!

- ❖ Intertwining their trunks is also a way of hugging for elephants. They are really social creatures who need love and affection all the time.

- ❖ Elephants' eyes are mostly small and brown.

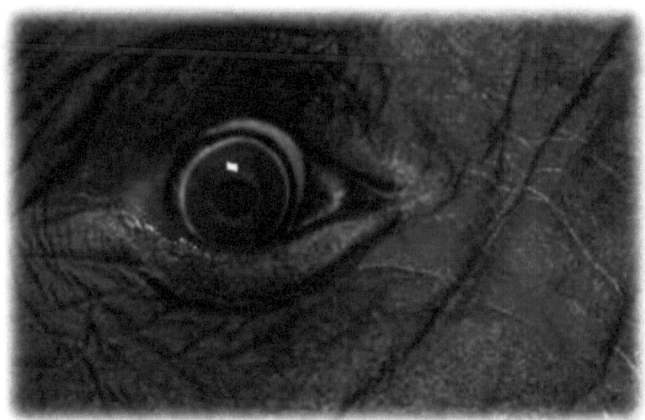

- ❖ Elephants can also swim far—this is also the reason why crocodiles are one of their worst enemies.

- ❖ Elephants walk on tiptoes—or by using the balls of their feet.

- ❖ The back of elephants' ears is the softest part of their bodies.

- ❖ An elephant's tail can grow as long as 1.3 meters.

- ❖ An elephant's tusks are actually overgrown teeth.

❖ It's not true that elephants get drunk by eating the fermented fruit of the marula tree. The fruit does not actually stay in their stomach for a long time and can easily pass through their intestines.

❖ Elephants flap their ears to show either joy or aggression. Their ears are also very useful as these help in protecting them against the harsh rays of the sun, especially in African savannahs.

❖ Lawrence Anthony, the so-called Elephant Whisperer, developed a great friendship with elephants throughout his lifetime. In fact, when he died, a herd of elephants went to his house to pay their respects and to mourn for him. When elephants do this, it means that they consider someone to be part of their family or at least, consider him as a friend.

- ❖ When an elephant gets sick, the tribe makes sure that they take care of it by bringing it food and helping it stand.

- ❖ When the elephant dies, the tribe will still try to give it food and when they realize that the elephant truly has died, they will spend some time being quiet. This is considered as their death ritual.

- ❖ After this moment of silence, they will then dig a grave for the elephant, covering it with branches and dirt. They will then stay beside the grave for a couple of days. Other elephant tribes that pass by also pay their respects.

AFRICAN ELEPHANTS

❖ Elephant brains are five times larger than human brains. Elephants are actually some of the most intelligent animals on Earth. They know how to show and understand happiness, sadness, grief, and playfulness. They also know how to be cooperative and friendly. They learn by observing what's going on around them and by mimicking what they think is right.

REFERENCES

http://animals.nationalgeographic.com/animals/mammals/african-elephant/

http://factsquest.blogspot.com/2013/01/elephant.html

http://listverse.com/2012/03/05/top-10-facts-about-elephants/

http://reidparkzoo.org/2011/06/10-fun-facts-about-african-elephants/

http://www.africapoint.com/blog/article/african-elephant-8-interesting-facts.html

http://www.animalfactguide.com/animal-facts/african-elephant/

http://www.ask.com/question/what-does-an-elephant-eat

http://www.ask.com/question/what-does-an-elephant-eat

http://www.ask.com/question/what-is-a-female-elephant-called

http://www.bestfunfacts.com/elephants.html

http://www.buzzle.com/articles/interesting-facts-about-elephants.html

http://www.conservenature.org/learn_about_wildlife/asian_elephant/male_elephants.htm

http://www.dailymail.co.uk/sciencetech/article-1308415/Elephants-NOT-afraid-mice-terrified-ants.html

http://www.factslides.com/s-Elephants

AFRICAN ELEPHANTS

http://www.huffingtonpost.com/2013/09/17/elephant-and-dog-bffs_n_3941832.html

http://www.jumbofoundation.com/facts-about-elephants.php

http://www.smithsonianmag.com/science-nature/14-fun-facts-about-elephants-14572816/?no-ist

http://www.smithsonianmag.com/science-nature/how-male-elephants-bond-64316480/

http://www.smithsonianmag.com/science-nature/what-in-the-world-is-a-rock-hyrax-89077364/

http://www.upali.ch/differences_en.html

http://www.woodall-addo.co.za/interesting-similarities-humans-elephants/

CONCLUSION

Thank you again for purchasing this book!

I hope you enjoyed reading about my book on African Elephants.

Finally, if you enjoyed this book, please take the time to share your thoughts and **post a review on Amazon**. It would be greatly appreciated!

Thank you!

A NOTE ABOUT THE AUTHOR:

Sean Liburd is a father, husband, entrepreneur, community builder, educator, listener and thinker. He is the founder and co-owner of Knowledge Bookstore which was established on December 18, 1997. Sean has learned that books educate and inform - but they also make you laugh, wonder and carry you to worlds you've never heard of inhabited by people you've never seen - a kaleidoscope of cultures painted on the pages in words, in pictures and in dreams. Books "Awaken the Mind" which is both Knowledge Bookstore's slogan and Sean's goal.

Feel free to contact Sean Liburd at sil@gmail.com

Check out my Amazon profile here:

www. amazon.com/author/seanliburd

CHECK OUT MY OTHER BOOK

Butterflies and Moths: All About Butterflies and Moths, A Kids Introduction to Butterflies and Moths Fun Facts and Fantastic Photos!

www.ingramcontent.com/pod-product-compliance
Lightning Source LLC
Chambersburg PA
CBHW050818290526
45792CB00001B/163